Health Zone

TAKE a Stand!

What YOU Can DO about BULLYING

Carrie Golus   illustrations by Jack Desrocher

Consultant Sonja Green, MD

Lerner Publications Company

Minneapolis

All characters in this book are fictional and are not based on actual persons. The characters' stories are not based on actual events. Any similarities thereof are purely coincidental.

Lerner Publications Company
A division of Lerner Publishing Group, Inc.
241 First Avenue North
Minneapolis, MN 55401 U.S.A.

Website address: www.lernerbooks.com

Library of Congress Cataloging-in-Publication Data

Golus, Carrie, 1969–
    Take a stand! : what you can do about bullying / by Carrie Golus ; illustrated by Jack Desrocher.
        p.   cm. — (Health zone)
    Includes bibliographical references (p. 61) and index.
    ISBN 978–0–8225–7554–2 (lib. bdg. : alk. paper)
    1. Bullying. I. Desrocher, Jack. II. Title.
    BF637.B85G65 2009
    302.3—dc22   2007049659

Manufactured in the United States of America
1 2 3 4 5 6 — BP — 14 13 12 11 10 09

Table of Contents

It was Tuesday again.
Adam HATED Tuesdays.
Every other day,

Adam's mom picked him up from school. But on Tuesdays, his mom had to work late. That meant Adam had to ride the bus.

Adam used to like riding the bus, before Charlie came along. Charlie was the new kid in school. But you would never know it. Most new kids took a while to figure out how they fit in.

But Charlie had come in and acted like he owned the place the first day.

Adam had never really cared about being popular.
He had a couple of good friends. He liked math and art and playing the guitar. But he wasn't cool by Charlie's standards. And now, every time Adam rode the bus, Charlie made sure to remind him of that.

Some days it was little things like throwing paper airplanes at his head. Other days, it was bigger stuff. One time, Charlie threw Adam's math book out the window. Most days, it was getting tripped or having Charlie yell rude things at him. Charlie really loved it when he could get the other kids to laugh. He thought he was so funny.

Some days, Adam felt so angry but didn't know what to do.
He didn't want to talk back to Charlie. That would only make the bullying worse. He didn't know what he had ever done to make Charlie hate him so much.

And he didn't know how much longer he could stand to just ignore it.

Chapter 1

WHAT IS Bullying?

When most people think of bullying, they think of physical attacks.

Hitting, shoving, tripping, or grabbing someone are all examples of bullying.

Bullying can include taking someone's backpack or other belongings. Or it can be forcing someone to hand over their money. Threatening to hurt someone counts as bullying too.

But there is much more to bullying than that. Bullying can also be completely nonphysical. It can mean calling someone names, spreading secrets, or leaving someone out of a group.

No one is sure exactly how common bullying is. One U.S. study found that 10 percent of students were victims of severe bullying. Another study found that 75 percent of children were bullied at least once during their school years. **If that's true, then three out of every four kids will be picked on before they're out of school.**

For some victims, the bullying starts with teasing and goes no further. But for others, the bullying gets worse over time. Other kids might join in. The teasing might turn into physical bullying.

BULLY #1 STOPPER

If you're being bullied, you're not alone! Seventy-five percent means more kids are bullied than not. So talk to your friends about it. Getting the problem out in the open is a first step to stopping the bully problem in your school.

Here are a few more ways bullying can be described:

The bully is more powerful than the target. (So if two people are equally powerful, it isn't bullying.)

Bullies can be either individuals or groups.

Targets can also be either individuals or groups.

Bullies choose targets they think they can control. They pick on people who won't be able to stand up for themselves.

A bully often goes after the same target again and again.

One sad fact is that most forms of bullying are not against the law. That doesn't mean bullying isn't serious. It just means that young people are treated differently from adults. If an adult pushed or hit someone, that would be called assault. Taking someone's belongings would be theft. Offending someone again and again would be called harassment.

But even if bullying among young people isn't illegal, it's still wrong.

Why Do Some Kids Bully?

One easy answer to why some kids bully is because it makes them feel strong and powerful. What's harder to explain is why these kids need to put others down to make themselves feel good.

One study found an interesting difference between most boy bullies and most girl bullies. Girl bullies tend to be popular, cool, and smart. Adults often see them as "good girls." Boy bullies tend to have fewer friends. They are less "cool," and they get lower grades than girl bullies. So the reason these boys bully may be to gain attention from others. For popular girls, bullying may be an attempt to feel more important.

Tom Cruise Was Bullied

Actor Tom Cruise attended fifteen different schools in twelve years. Small for his age, he was often the target of bullies. Cruise hated fighting. But he learned that he had to fight back or else the bully would pick on him all year.

Eminem Turns the Tables on a Bully

In the 1999 song "Brain Damage," rapper Eminem wrote about a real-life bully, D'Angelo Bailey. Bailey had bullied Eminem in school. Later, Bailey tried to sue Eminem for harming his reputation. Bailey admitted the bullying. But he said it was not as bad as Eminem's song suggested. Bailey lost the case.

Boy and girl bullies might be different. But whether kids are popular or not, they still could have self-esteem problems. And low self-esteem could cause someone to bully.

Sometimes, bullies may not understand how much their behavior hurts their victims. Most kids say that teasing counts as bullying. However, some bullies argue that their teasing isn't serious. They think victims should be able to just brush it off. Bullies often say they do it just for fun.

Some think that bullies' parents are to blame because they neglect their children. That may cause the children to bully others in hopes of getting some attention. Or some kids may bully because they are victims of physical abuse at home.

Bullies may have lots of reasons for the mean things they do. But none of those reasons makes their behavior okay.

Chapter 2

WHAT THE
Experts
SAY

In the 1970s,

a professor named Dan Olweus was studying bullying. He was one of the first to point out that bullying *is not* just an ordinary part of childhood.

It is ABUSE.

This was a completely new way to think about bullying.

A lot more studying has been done since then. But we don't have all the answers yet. We do know that bullying really is a big deal. It can cause long-term suffering. Some adults who were severely bullied as children still find it hard to trust people. They still feel sad about the bullying, years after it stopped.

In the United States, bullying was not taken very seriously until the 1990s. Unfortunately, it took a series of school shootings to make Americans realize how harmful bullying can be. After nearly every school shooting, it was discovered that the shooter had been severely bullied.

School shootings have brought national attention to the bullying problem. However, these cases are very unusual. It's okay to stand up to a bully in a fair way. But it's never okay to choose violence. Bringing a gun to school is never a way to solve a problem. The good news is that victims who want to fight back rarely become this violent. The bad news is that most victims never speak up or fight back at all.

The Power of Bystanders

Many people don't realize that bullying is a group activity. Bullying almost always happens when other kids are around. The way these bystanders act can make a huge difference.

Some students see bullying but don't do anything to stop it. This makes the bully think his or her behavior is okay. Olweus has called people who stand by and do nothing to stop the bullying "passive bullies." They seem to approve of the bully's actions. That's a type of bullying in itself.

At lunch one day, Zach was eating a candy bar. Chris grabbed it out of Zach's hand. Then Chris shoved the whole thing in his mouth. When Zach got mad, Chris grabbed his soda too. No one at the cafeteria table said anything. Some even laughed.

Sometimes, bystanders may join in the bullying just to go along with the group. The bystanders might do mean things they would never ordinarily do. Sometimes it's easy to think that if an entire group of kids is acting in a certain way, then there isn't anything wrong with it.

Hannah was walking down the hall when she saw a group of girls knock Sydney's books out of her arms. Sydney was trying not to cry as she picked them up. Hannah laughed and kicked one of the books across the hallway. Then she and another girl started playing soccer with it.

In one study, kids were videotaped together on a playground. It showed that 85 percent of bullying situations happened in front of other kids. Most of the time, the bystanders either joined in the bullying or just watched. **Bystanders tried to stop the bullying only about 10 percent of the time.**

Later, the bystanders were asked why they hadn't tried to step in and stop the bullying. They had many different reasons:

They were embarrassed.

They didn't know what to do.

They were busy doing something else.

They were afraid they would be next.

They were afraid the bully would get back at them later.

They weren't sure if the teacher would back them up or not.

BULLY #2 STOPPER

Be bold enough to step in and protect another kid. Talk to your teachers and counselors about forming a "bully-stopper" team. These students can learn the best and safest ways to stop being a passive bully.

When someone is bullied, it affects how the other kids see both the bully and the victim. The bully often gains power and respect from the other students. The victim loses both power and respect. This is because he or she appears weak to the others. It shouldn't be this way, but studies have shown that it's true. When bullying happens over and over, other kids can develop a low opinion of the victim. They may even think the victim deserves to be bullied.

In order for bullying to end, bystanders have to stop encouraging the bully. At some schools, kids who aren't either bullies or victims have been trained to step in and help.

Kaitlyn saw Hannah and Danielle kicking Sydney's book back and forth. Instead of walking by, Kaitlyn grabbed the book and gave it back to Sydney. Then Kaitlyn asked Sydney if she was okay and gave her a hug. When the other girls saw what Kaitlyn was doing, one of them said, "Sorry. We were just having fun."

Can Teachers and Schools Make Bullying Worse?

Believe it or not, bullying isn't just a problem brought on by kids. Teachers, the principal, and other people who work at the school also play a part.

Bullying is most common during times when there aren't a lot of adults around. This is usually at lunch, before and after class, and at recess. Even if kids are by themselves for just a short time, bullying tends to increase.

Bullies usually try to hide their behavior from adults. Sometimes teachers don't know it's going on. And neither victims nor bystanders are likely to tell the teacher about bullying. Victims often feel too embarrassed to say anything. And nobody wants to be thought of as a tattletale.

Physical bullying is easier for teachers to pick up on. But bullying can be much less noticeable than that. It's harder for a busy teacher to notice kids telling secrets or leaving someone out of a group.

Adults usually take physical bullying more seriously. But in one study, kids said that teasing actually hurt more. The old rhyme "Sticks and stones may break my bones but words can never hurt me" is simply not true.

If teachers ignore bullying and don't take action, the bullying may get worse. Sometimes, teachers don't stop the bullying even if a student asks for help.

Jeremy and Richard often called Haley mean names and made fun of her. One day in the hall, they took her gym shoes and threw them in the trash. Haley asked her teacher, Ms. Reece, for help. Ms. Reece said Haley should just play along. She said Jeremy and Richard probably just had a crush on her.

Even worse, some teachers actually encourage bullying among their students. You can probably think of at least one teacher like this at your school. He or she may seem more concerned with popularity than with teaching.

Jesse hated gym. He tried his best in sports like soccer and field hockey. But his teacher often yelled mean stuff like, "My grandma moves faster than that!" Sometimes Jesse's classmates joined in on the shouting. They called him names and shoved him during class. Jesse's teacher did nothing to stop the teasing.

If a teacher is bullying you, get help from someone else. Tell a school counselor, the principal, or a different teacher you trust. Other adults need to know what's happening so it can be stopped.

It's not just some teachers who contribute to bullying. Strange as it may sound, school buildings themselves may be part of the problem. Some schools have lots of hidden areas where it is hard for a teacher to see what's going on. Any place in school where there are kids but no adults is a place where bullying might happen.

Another problem is that some school yards don't have much for kids to do. Without games or stuff to play on, bored students turn to bullying. Bullying is less common at schools with fun playgrounds. It also helps if the teachers organize games or activities. That keeps the kids too busy playing to pick on one another.

Bullying is a problem when older and younger children have recess together. Even the length of the recess can encourage bullying. You might think it's great if your school has a long break. But bullying is worse at the end of an hour-long recess. When kids get bored or when they have smaller kids to pick on, they bully more.

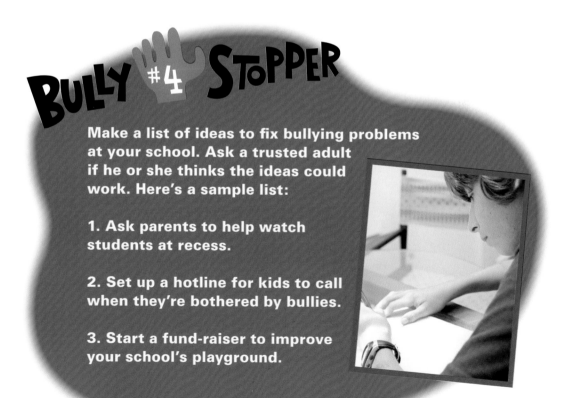

BULLY #4 STOPPER

Make a list of ideas to fix bullying problems at your school. Ask a trusted adult if he or she thinks the ideas could work. Here's a sample list:

1. Ask parents to help watch students at recess.

2. Set up a hotline for kids to call when they're bothered by bullies.

3. Start a fund-raiser to improve your school's playground.

Victims One Day, Bullies the Next

The truth is most kids aren't just bullies or just victims. It's not that simple. Some kids can be bullies in one situation and victims in another. They are called bully-victims.

Logan was often picked on by a group of boys at school. After school his younger neighbor Sean wanted to play basketball with Logan and his friends. Logan said no and threw the ball at Sean's head.

Bully-victims turn to bullying to vent anger over being bullied themselves. You might think that kids who have been bullied wouldn't do it to others. After all, they know it hurts. But bully-victims are not able to put themselves in their victim's shoes. Instead, they enjoy the feeling of power that comes from being a bully for a change.

Luckily, not all victims of bullying become bullies themselves. Some kids who were bullied when they were younger are strongly against any kind of bullying. These kids are more likely to step in to try to stop bullying.

Experts on bullying now think even the idea of bully-victim is too simple. Instead, we should think of bullying as a straight line. Bullies are on one end, and victims are on the other. Most kids (and adults) would fall somewhere in the middle.

BULLY #5 STOPPER

Stop the bully chain! If you find yourself picking on your sister, your neighbor, or your best friend, think about why you are. Did someone tease you earlier that day? Find another way to feel powerful. Ride your bike up a hill. Work on a hard math puzzle. Or teach your little sister some new soccer skills.

Chapter 3

FRIENDS OR Bullies?

There is an old myth that
bullying
is done mostly by boys.

If you're a girl, you know that just isn't the case.

Girls can be really mean too.

They just do it differently.

Until about the age of four, girls and boys hurt other kids in the same way. Little girls hit, push, and grab toys just as little boys do. When they get older, boy bullies still bully others that way. They usually bully kids they have never been friends with.

Older girls sometimes bully by hitting or pushing. And they sometimes bully kids who aren't their friends. *But girls usually pick on friends, ex-friends, or girls who want to be their friends*. The ways girls bully may be less noticeable than the punches or kicks boy bullies deliver. Girl bullies may roll their eyes. They might shoot dirty looks. They could turn their backs to shut someone out of the group.

This is called **relational bullying**—bullying by trying to hurt other girls' relationships. Relational bullying includes a lot of different behavior. It can mean telling secrets or spreading lies. It can mean trying to turn someone's friends against her. It can mean leaving someone out—for example, inviting the whole class to a party except for one girl. Or it can mean making friends with someone just to hurt someone else.

Can Boys be Relational Bullies?

It does happen. But studies have shown that boys and girls usually bully differently. True, boys call one another mean names, just like girls do. But boys tend to be rougher and more physical, both when they're playing and when they're bullying. Boys are more likely than girls to hurt their victims physically.

The typical boy bully is bigger and stronger than most other boys in his class. He also tends to be bossier. He likes to pick on other boys just for fun. A boy bully likes knowing that other kids are scared of him. He doesn't feel sorry for his victims.

A boy bully will often search out boys who are smaller and who don't like to play rough. The ideal target is someone who will take the bullying day after day and not say anything. The bully will try to get his friends to bully the victim too. In really bad cases, an entire class turns on the target.

Cliques and Bullying

A clique is a small circle of friends. You may not use that word, but you definitely know what a clique is. The popular crowd is a clique. There are lots of other cliques too. They are often formed around common interests, like music or sports or what neighborhood you're from. Having a close group of friends can be a good thing because it gives you a sense of belonging. But a clique tends to set rules for who can and can't belong. That's when trouble starts.

Cliques are most common during the middle school years. This can make an already stressful time even worse. Everyone is under a lot of pressure to fit in to a new school with lots of new people.

All too often, that pressure can lead to bullying. Bullying tends to be a group activity, mainly with girls. In a clique, girls may do mean things they would never do on their own.

Karleen had one popular friend, Natalie. Karleen wanted to be friends with the other popular girls. One day, Natalie and the others were talking about how much they hated Jasmine. Karleen had always liked Jasmine. But she pretended she hated Jasmine too. She even made up a mean song about her.

Kate Winslet Was Bullied

As a child, British actress Kate Winslet was bullied for being overweight and having large feet. In 1997, Winslet starred in the film *Titanic*, which won eleven Academy Awards.

Bullying can also happen because cliques change so often. The popular crowd suddenly finds room for a new member. Or just as suddenly, they kick someone out. Girls who were best friends can become terrible enemies. From sixth to eighth grade, it can be very hard to know who your friends are.

BULLY #6 STOPPER

For boys, it can be tough if you're not good at sports. But everyone is good at something. You just have to find what it is. Martial arts, like karate or aikido, are a good choice. Martial arts are about skill, not about strength or size. They are about defending yourself, not hurting others. If you're sure of yourself, a bully is less likely to pick on you.

from friend to Target

It's hard when an old friend starts hanging out with a new crowd. This is especially true if the new friends aren't very nice. You might wonder why your old friend has changed so much. You might wonder if losing her friendship was somehow your fault.

When a friendship ends, it's usually not because of something either friend did. It's because girls' interests change, and they become curious about new people and things. Unfortunately, as girls try to figure out who they are, they sometimes forget who they used to be. Some girls hope that by bullying their ex-friends they will gain new friends.

Anna and Kelsey were best friends in elementary school. But in junior high, Kelsey became friends with Olivia. Whenever Kelsey was with Olivia, she either made fun of Anna or completely ignored her. Anna couldn't understand what she had done to make Kelsey suddenly hate her.

Girls love to share secrets with one another. That makes girls the best friends and the worst enemies. An ex-friend can be the meanest enemy of all.

Race, Girls, and Bullying

Research has found that friend-on-friend bullying may be worse among white girls. African American or Latina girls are less likely to put up with bad treatment from their friends.

In sixth grade, Jennifer's best friend Madison started hanging out with the popular crowd. Madison told her new friends all of Jennifer's secrets—like her crush on Mr. Beasley, the math teacher. Afterward, all the popular girls started calling Jennifer "Mrs. Beasley." They even did it in math class, where he could hear them.

Sometimes, an old friend is mean in public but nice in private. An old friend might ignore you or even tease you at school. But then she might call you on the weekend as if nothing were wrong. Unfortunately, many girls put up with this treatment. They miss their old friend and hope she'll start being nicer. They would rather have a broken friendship than none at all. But beware. This isn't a part-time friendship. *It's abuse.*

When the Bullies Are Your Friends

A lot of girls think if only they could be popular, life would be perfect. But believe it or not, bullying is often worse within the popular crowd.

Sometimes, the popular girls bully outsiders. But more often, they bully other members of the clique—girls who are supposed to be their friends.

Cliques have certain rules for how the members behave. If you break the rules, you can become a target of bullying. Something as simple as wearing pants on the day everyone agreed to wear a skirt could give a bully something to bully about.

Meghan always sat with the popular girls at lunch. Nearly every day, the other girls made fun of her. They teased her about her hair, her eating habits, her good grades—just about anything.

Once Meghan tried to tell her friends how much the teasing bothered her. The other girls acted mad and said they were only joking. Meghan said she was sorry for making a big deal about it. But she was still upset.

Teasing puts the target in her place—below the teaser. Unfortunately, trying to fight back against the clique usually doesn't work. Often the target ends up saying sorry, and sometimes the teasing gets worse.

Many girls in this situation don't even realize they're being bullied. They don't want to believe their friends really want to hurt them. They might feel like they are somehow to blame. They put up with it because they want to be popular or they don't want to lose their friends.

There can be long-term effects of being a victim of relational bullying. When these girls grow up, they may be more likely to put up with abuse from others. They have come to believe that being bullied is just part of life.

Girls who aren't popular sometimes have the healthiest friendships and the highest self-esteem. You wouldn't think it, but not being popular actually might be a good thing.

BULLY #7 STOPPER

If the kids in your clique are giving you a hard time, think twice about belonging. Is it worth all the teasing? You shouldn't allow yourself to be the running joke of the group. Let your friends know it bugs you. And don't back down. If that doesn't stop the bullying, then let these friends go.

Chapter 4

CYBER-Bullying

SCHOOL-YARD BULLIES used to be just that. They were bullies who bothered their victims at school.

Then came the Internet and cell phones.

Now bullies can keep picking on their targets long after the school day is over. The problem has become so common, it even has its own term—*cyberbullying.* It's also known as online bullying, Internet bullying, or electronic bullying.

Between one-third and one-fifth of kids have been cyberbullied. Just as most victims of regular bullying don't tell an adult, most victims of cyberbullying keep their problem a secret.

Being bullied in person is scary. Being bullied online or by cell phone can be even scarier. It feels like there's no escape. Here are just a few examples of what can happen.

Mean e-mails or instant messages
Tyler got an e-mail from someone called "Guess Who?" The message said everyone at school hated him.

Web pages set up to make fun of someone
A group of girls created a website for the "We All Hate Elizabeth" club.

People pretending to be someone else online
John was able to get into Andrew's e-mail account by guessing his password. He signed into Andrew's account and sent a rude e-mail to a girl he knew Andrew liked.

Embarrassing photos or videos
Ryan felt sick at school and threw up in the hallway before he could make it to the bathroom. James took a photo with his cell phone, and within minutes, the whole school knew about it.

Private e-mails forwarded without permission
Brianna was sad because she and Lauren weren't friends anymore. When she sent Lauren a sad e-mail about it, Lauren added some mean comments and forwarded it to all her new friends.

Bad behavior in online groups
Annalise asked all of her friends to block Courtney from their friendship lists.

Online voting sites used to publicly embarrass others
A group of kids set up a site where they and others could vote for the ugliest, weirdest, and most unpopular person at school.

Cyberstalking (using e-mail or the Internet to bother or threaten someone again and again)
Kevin was angry when Amber broke up with him. He sent her hundreds of e-mails. When Amber didn't write back, Kevin sent her computer viruses and tried to hack into her computer.

Unfortunately, technology has made it possible to bully people in all kinds of new and different ways. Worse yet, some kids who would never be bullies in real life think it's okay to bully people online. Maybe they don't take it seriously. Or maybe they don't think they'll get caught. But cyberbullying isn't just a game. The consequences are very real for the victims.

BULLY #8 STOPPER

Don't choose passwords or user names that would be easy for other people to guess. If you get cyberbullied, keep the messages in case you need to prove what happened.

password
julie

JULIE

How Is Cyberbullying Different from Regular Bullying?

In many ways, cyberbullying is just another form of relational bullying. You can't hurt someone physically with a computer or cell phone. But you can certainly hurt someone's feelings and make them feel scared and unsafe.

Cyberbullying has some important differences from ordinary bullying, though. **The Internet makes it much easier for bullies to be anonymous (to keep their name secret).** Bullies can set up secret e-mail accounts or use fake names in chat rooms. When bullies bother their victims anonymously, they sometimes do or say mean things that they wouldn't face-to-face.

At school, bullying increases when kids aren't as closely watched. On the Internet, there is often no one watching. (Some chat rooms have people who keep an eye on what's being written. But no one is checking e-mails, instant messages, and most websites.) Young people are often better at using computers and cell phones than their parents are. So kids can use a computer or cell phone to bully others without worrying they'll get caught.

Finally, cyberbullying is quick and easy. In just a few minutes, a cyberbully can fire off an ugly e-mail or post a hurtful comment on someone's blog. On the Internet, everything happens so fast. Cyberbullies may not stop and think before they act. And once they hit "send," they can't go back.

Who Are the Cyberbullies?

Some cyberbullies are also bullies in real life. The Internet and cell phones are just powerful tools that let them keep bothering their victims.

But you don't have to be big, strong, powerful, or popular to be a cyberbully. You just have to have some computer skills and some time on your hands.

Some cyberbullies are bully-victims, those who have been picked on by others. They might be as young as seven or eight years old. In real life, they would never dare to pick on others. But online, they can be very powerful and use technology as a way to fight back.

The difference between victims and bullies is less clear in the online world. Often, when kids are bullied online, they try to bully back. Kids can go from victim to bully and back again.

Haley wrote an embarrassing secret about Erin on her blog. Erin got back at her by posting Haley's phone number online and encouraging boys to call her. Erin knew that would get Haley in trouble with her mom.

How Serious Is Cyberbullying?

Sometimes bullying breaks the rules (usually called terms of service) of a website or an Internet service provider (ISP). For example, one popular video-sharing site states that if a video shows someone getting hurt or embarrassed, it shouldn't be posted. But these rules are often broken and nothing happens. Most companies don't have time to make sure everyone follows these rules. Many cyberbullies think what they're doing is no big deal. And they assume they won't get caught.

What many kids don't realize is that cyberbullying can be against the law. In the United States, it is a crime to anonymously threaten or bother anyone by Internet or phone. Hacking and stealing passwords can also be serious crimes. For kids with technical skills, these things are easy. But just because it's easy doesn't mean it's okay.

Brian thought it was funny to send anonymous threats to a teacher he didn't like. His teacher didn't find it so funny. Neither did Brian's parents when the police arrived at the door.

BULLY #9 STOPPER

Never ignore something as serious as a death threat or a bomb threat. If you receive one, tell an adult right away and let the police know what happened.

Boys, Girls, and Cyberbullying

Girls and boys tend to cyberbully differently, just as they tend to bully differently in real life. Girls share personal information about their victims online. Or they write mean e-mails or instant messages. Boys pass around hurtful photos, hack into other kids' computers, and steal passwords.

Chapter 5

HOW DO WE SOLVE THE Bullying Problem?

Bullying is a really challenging problem, and there's no easy fix.

But it is possible to take a stand. So if you're being bullied,

don't give up.

First, remember the bullying is not your fault. You did nothing to bring it on, no matter what the bully says. Maybe you're different from the other kids in some way. Whatever. It doesn't matter why you're being bullied. *No one* deserves to be bullied.

Second, it's not your responsibility to fix the problem by yourself. Don't forget that bullying isn't just about the bully and the victim. Bystanders, teachers, and parents need to help too. It's up to everybody to help stop bullies.

Just telling a bully to stop sometimes works. But you can never be sure what might happen. You have to be prepared for anything. Letting a bully know how you feel might get him or her to back off. Or it might just make the bullying worse.

What about fighting back physically? *(Hey, it worked for Tom Cruise.)* This is a risky game, and it usually works better in the movies than in real life. You could get hurt. And you might get in trouble if a teacher catches you. It might look like you're part of the problem instead of the victim.

Sometimes you feel you have to say or do something to stand up for yourself. But you also need to think about what's safe. Some bullies can turn violent. It's more important to take the safe route than to take risks. You'll have reason to be proud if you don't sink to the bully's level. **The hard truth is that it's almost impossible to stop bullying without some kind of help.** *So ask for help!*

Anti-Bullying Programs in Schools

Find out if your school has an anti-bullying program. Ask your counselor or principal to look at Olweus's program. His suggestions include:

- having teachers talk and play games with students at recess and at lunch

- holding a school-wide assembly on the subject of bullying

- having class meetings about how to get along, including mock bullying situations

- gathering students for small-group projects and fun activities to build respect for others

Breaking the Silence

Bullying happens because of a "code of silence." No one tells. Bullies usually try to hide their behavior from teachers and other adults. Bystanders don't want to be thought of as tattletales, so they don't say anything. And victims often feel embarrassed to admit they're being bullied. (Don't be embarrassed—it's the bully who should be embarrassed about acting that way!) Remember, 75 percent of kids will be bullied at some point during their school years. That means you are definitely not the only one.

So the first thing you should do is tell someone. If you have a friend you trust, start by talking to him or her. And stick together. If you have a friend with you, the bully might leave you alone. Your friend also might be able to stand up for you. But even if your friend can't give you any help or advice, it often helps just to share your problems. Bullies try to make you feel alone, and it helps to know that you're not.

What if the bullying doesn't stop or if your friends aren't nearby when the bullying happens? Try talking to a trusted adult. It could be your mom or dad, a teacher, or the school counselor. If the first adult you talk to doesn't help, go to someone else. *Keep trying until you find someone who will listen and help.*

Confronting the Bully:
CHELSEA'S STORY

Chelsea was thrilled when she was chosen for the lead in the school play. But Tiffany was used to being the star of the show. She was furious that she had gotten only a small part.

Tiffany told all the other girls in the cast that Chelsea got the best part because she was teacher's pet. At practice, none of the girls would speak to Chelsea. If she forgot her lines, they all laughed. During the break, they whispered and made fun of her.

The teasing made Chelsea so upset she thought about quitting the play.

Chelsea asked her favorite aunt for advice. Aunt Yvette told Chelsea to make friends with some of the kids who weren't bullying her. She also said Chelsea should talk to Tiffany alone. Chelsea practiced what she would say. If those things didn't work, Aunt Yvette said, Chelsea should talk to the drama teacher.

The next morning, Chelsea talked to Tiffany. She got through it by using her acting skills—she pretended she was braver than she was! She told Tiffany she didn't like the teasing and asked her to stop. Tiffany just said, "Whatever," and walked away. But Chelsea felt good that she had stood up for herself.

Chelsea decided she didn't want to talk to the drama teacher about it. Instead, she made it a point to be friendly to the guys in the cast. When the art club came to paint sets, Chelsea hung out with them. The more friends Chelsea had around her, the less Tiffany picked on her. The bullying didn't stop completely. But Chelsea was glad she hadn't quit. The best part was that she made some new friends.

Avoiding the Bully:
ADAM'S STORY

Sometimes, like Chelsea, you don't just avoid a bully. Other times, it's not a bad idea to.

Avoiding the bully worked for Adam—remember Adam? He was the one who was bullied by Charlie on the school bus.

When Adam finally told his dad about what was happening, he was really supportive. Adam's dad joked that Charlie sounded like a real grouch and should go back to his garbage can. Adam rolled his eyes at his dad's dumb joke. But somehow, it still made him feel better.

Adam's dad had a good idea about the bus problem. He suggested that Adam take guitar lessons on Tuesday afternoons. He could walk there from school. Then Adam's dad could pick him up after work. Adam wouldn't have to ride the bus anymore.

Adam was lucky. He didn't have any classes with Charlie. He was able to avoid the bully completely, and the bullying stopped.

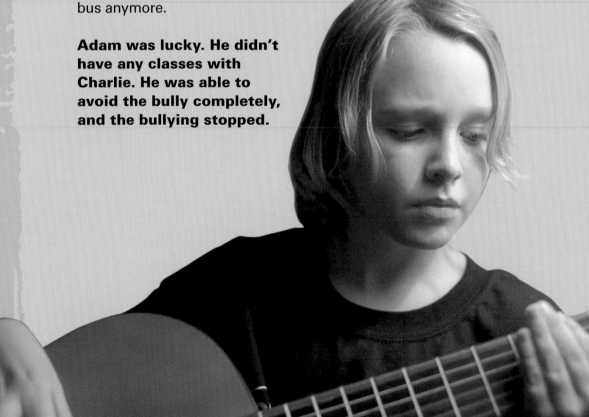

What If You're Being Cyberbullied?

In some ways, cyberbullying can be easier to deal with than face-to-face bullying. If you're being bullied in a certain chat room, for example, you can change your user name. Or you can just quit going there. If you're being bullied by e-mail, you can change your address or block the sender.

Unlike other forms of bullying, cyberbullying can sometimes be stopped if you ignore it. If you don't reply, the bully never knows whether you got his mean e-mail or not.

You don't have to read a cyberbully's messages. But you shouldn't delete them either. If the cyberbully still won't leave you alone, you can report him to his Internet service provider. If you can show that you're being cyberbullied, the ISP might close his account.

When Bullies Grow Up

According to one study, child bullies are more likely to have problems with violence when they grow up. One in four bullies has a criminal record by the age of 30.

Getting the School Involved:
JASON'S STORY

Jason was one of the outsiders at school. But he didn't really care. He had a few close friends that he liked to hang out with. He also had a lot of online friends, even some in different countries.

Jason was a good writer, and he started writing a daily blog about life at his junior high. At first, only Jason's friends read it. But as word spread about how funny it was, lots of other kids started reading it too.

But not everyone found it so funny. He started getting mean e-mails. Usually they were anonymous or under fake names. Jason tried not to let the bullies bother him. He never wrote back. He just blocked the senders.

But the cyberbullying got worse. There was one bully who wouldn't stop. Jason figured out who it was—Kyle, a guy in his science class.

Jason was pretty sure Kyle was just messing around. But when Kyle started making death threats, he finally felt scared. He decided to talk to the school counselor, Mr. Johnson.

Mr. Johnson took Jason's problem very seriously. He called Kyle, Jason, and their parents in to a meeting. Mr. Johnson explained that the school couldn't punish Kyle because he had not used a school computer to send the e-mails. But Mr. Johnson also made it clear that Kyle had broken the law. Even if he never meant to follow through on the threats, it was still illegal. After the meeting, Kyle never bullied Jason again.

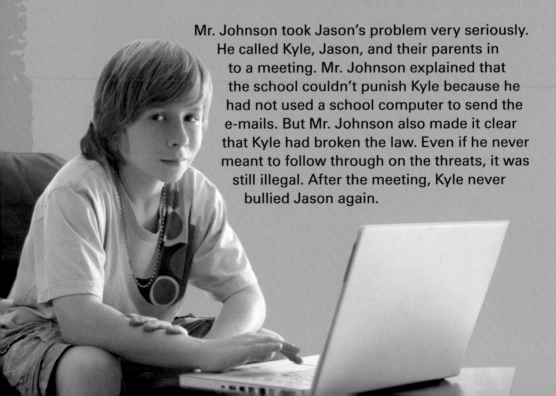

When Bullying Is Extreme

Sometimes bullying can get completely out of hand.
When bullying is very bad or goes on for a long time, victims
can develop serious health problems. Some victims suffer from
depression or anxiety. Or they may develop eating disorders.

*Others try to deal with the issue by hurting
themselves.* Sometimes kids think they can make the pain
go away by cutting—slicing their skin with sharp objects. Sadly,
some victims try to kill themselves.

*In rare cases, bullying may lead to school
violence.* Sometimes even very young children bring guns
or other weapons to school to try to fight back.

Columbine Shootings

One of the worst school shootings was at Colorado's Columbine High School in 1999. Twenty-four people were hurt, and thirteen people were killed. The shooters, Eric Harris and Dylan Klebold, then killed themselves. No one knows exactly why Eric and Dylan did what they did. But many think they were trying to "get even" for the years of bullying they had suffered.

Sometimes a victim is being abused by so many bullies that the situation feels hopeless. If the bullying is so bad you want to hurt yourself or others, *get help right away.* Talk to your family, and let them know you can't take it anymore.

If you are suffering from severe bullying, there are ways to get yourself out of the situation. You could change homerooms. You could change schools. You could even ask your parents if you could be home-schooled for a while.

If it's a matter of life and death, this kind of change is not making too big a deal out of the problem. *It's absolutely necessary.*

Leaving the Bully Behind:
JOSH'S STORY

Josh hated walking to school in the morning. Bullies made his life completely rotten. They followed him, teased him, and sometimes threw his homework into rain gutters. Josh's grades had dropped because the bullies had destroyed so many of his assignments.

School was no better. He was tackled, pushed, and tripped in the hallways. His locker was broken into. He couldn't count a single friend in any of his classes.

Josh tried to get out of going to school as much as he could. He felt sick every morning because he was so scared. But usually, his mom made him go.

Josh didn't know what to do or why he was the one the bullies picked on. Sometimes he thought about bringing his stepfather's gun to school. Other times, he thought about using the gun on himself. But usually, he didn't think about very much. He just tried to get through the day.

One night, Josh started crying while talking to his father long-distance. He had never told anyone about the bullying before. But now, the truth came pouring out.

Josh's parents decided that Josh should go live with his dad for a while. Josh enrolled in an alternative school, which was different from most schools. There weren't as many students, and kids called the teachers by their first names. Josh was amazed to find the other kids were friendly and easygoing.

At first, Josh wasn't sure if he could really trust the other kids. But slowly, he opened up. By the end of the year, he was making As and Bs. He had joined the school track team. And he had two new best friends.

Bullying doesn't last forever.

If you're living with bullying, it might help to remember that it doesn't last forever. Bullying peaks in middle school and then goes down in later grades.

As they get older, most kids find a group of friends they're comfortable with. People grow up a little bit and stop getting thrills out of picking on others. Bullying still happens, but it's not so common or so painful.

It can be hard to see the light at the end of the tunnel if you're being bullied.

But remember, the bullying will end.

Your life will get better.

It all starts with taking a stand.

Quiz

Now that you've read all about bullying,

try this fun quiz to see how much you know. Please write your answers on a separate sheet of paper. (Answers appear at the bottom of page 58.)

1. **Which of the following is *not* an example of cyberbullying?**

   a. forwarding all your friends an e-mail in which another friend revealed her secret crush

   b. sending the latest supercolossal, nightmare computer virus to your ex-best friend

   c. convincing your entire class to block the new kid from their friendship lists

   d. decorating your home computer's desktop with a photo of you and your next-door neighbor dressed in goofy Halloween costumes

2. **One good way to deal with a cyberbully might be to:**

   a. ignore any mean texts or e-mails the cyberbully sends— but also save them in case you need to prove what happened

   b. start a Web page on which you post nasty rumors about the cyberbully

   c. order twenty sardine-and-anchovy pizzas from QuikPizzasToGo.com and have them delivered to the cyberbully's doorstep

   d. immediately delete any e-mails or texts you receive from the cyberbully

3. **How is cyberbullying different from real-world bullying?**

   a. a cyberbully can keep his identity secret

   b. a cyberbully doesn't have to be bigger or stronger than the victim

c. a cyberbully sometimes doesn't even realize he's bullying someone

d. all of the above

4. Which of these is not another term for cyberbullying?

a. online bullying

b. Internet bullying

c. electronic bullying

d. cyborg bullying

5. What online communication is supervised by adults?

a. e-mails

b. instant messages

c. some chat rooms

d. none of the above

6. What should you do if you send a mean e-mail to your ex-best friend and, an hour later, you wish you hadn't?

a. send the e-mail to five other friends asking if you should have sent it or not

b. call or go over to your ex-best friend's house and apologize

c. send your ex-friend another e-mail threatening what will happen if your ex-best friend reads the first one

d. pretend that someone else broke into your account and sent the e-mail

7. What kind of people are most likely to be cyberbullies?

a. popular girls, because they can't get enough of picking on their victims

b. unpopular boys, because they like to get revenge on real-world bullies

c. there is no typical cyberbully. All kinds of kids cyberbully—in all kinds of ways, for all kinds of reasons.

d. retired people, because they have a lot of free time to cause trouble

8. **Which of these examples is not just cyberbullying but a crime in the United States?**

    a. hacking into someone's computer

    b. sending someone a death threat or bomb threat

    c. stealing someone's password

    d. all of the above

9. **Your girlfriend is setting up a bash site where you can vote for the "biggest losers" at school. You're good at computers so she asks you to help. What should you do?**

    a. go ahead and help. It's no big deal, and she is your girlfriend.

    b. don't help and don't vote for anyone, but check the site every once in a while out of curiosity

    c. ask your girlfriend if it's really such a good idea. How would she feel if someone set up a website to make fun of her?

    d. pretend to help but secretly build lots of mistakes into the website's design so the site won't work very well

MY BULLYING JOURNAL

If you're being bullied, it sometimes helps to write about it. Who has been bullying you? Or do you think you might sometimes be the bully? In either case, what happened? How did it make you feel? Try writing about your feelings. Be sure to keep your journal somewhere safe and private. Also remember to note the date in each entry.

Keeping a journal can be particularly helpful if you think a friend might be bullying you. After you write about it, set your journal aside. After a few days, reread what you wrote, imagining it had happened to someone else. Is that the way friends are supposed to treat one another?

You might want to keep your journal just for yourself. Or you might want to share it with an adult you trust. This can be especially helpful if you think a friend is bullying you but aren't completely sure.

Writing in a journal doesn't just help you feel better. It is also a record of what happened when. If you decide to talk to a teacher, counselor, or principal, your journal might be useful. It can serve as written evidence of how serious the bullying is and how long it's been going on.

Glossary

abuse: harmful, wrong, or unfair treatment

anonymous: not named or identified

assault: a violent attack

blog: an online journal for all to read. *Blog* is short for weblog.

bystanders: people who are present but don't take part in an event

clique: a small circle of friends

computer virus: a computer program that can harm or destroy a computer

cyberstalking: using the Internet to bother or threaten someone again and again

hack: to break into someone's computer

harassment: regularly bothering or threatening someone

passive bullies: people who see bullying but do nothing to stop it

relational bullying: hurting people by harming their friendships or connections to others

self-esteem: the value or respect one places in oneselfs

Byrne, Brendan. *Coping with Bullying in Schools.* London: Cassell, 1994.

Geffner, Robert A., Marti Loring, and Corinna Young, eds. *Bullying Behavior: Current Issues, Research, and Interventions.* New York: Haworth Maltreatment & Trauma Press, 2001.

National Crime Prevention Council. "Cyerbullying." NCPC. 2007. http://www.ncpc.org/media/Cyberbullying.php (October 31, 2007).

Olweus, Dan. *Bullying at School: What We Know and What We Can Do.* Oxford, UK: Blackwell Publishers, 1993.

Patchin, Justin W., and Sameer Hinduja. "Bullies Move Beyond the Schoolyard: A Preliminary Look at Cyberbullying." *Youth Violence and Juvenile Justice,* 4, no. 2 (2006) 148–169.

Rigby, Ken. *New Perspectives on Bullying.* London: Jessica Kingsley, 2002.

Simmons, Rachel. *Odd Girl Out: The Hidden Culture of Aggression in Girls.* New York: Harcourt, 2002.

WiredKids. *Stop Cyberbullying.* N.d. http://www.stopcyberbullying.org (October 31, 2007).

Wiseman, Rosalind. *Queen Bees and Wannabes: Helping Your Daughter Survive Cliques, Gossip, Boyfriends and Other Realities of Adolescence.* New York: Three Rivers Press, 2002.

Learn More about Bullying

Blume, Judy. *Blubber.* New York: Dell Yearling, 2004.
Jill enjoys joining in on group bullying of an overweight girl in her class—until she becomes the bullies' next target.

Don't Tease Hotline
http://www.dontbullyhotline.com
This site is committed to educating kids about their rights and providing information on how to handle bullies.

It's My Life
http://www.pbskids.org/itsmylife/index.html
This website offers useful information on friends, family, health, emotions, and other topics.

Pacer Center Kids Against Bullying
http://www.pacerkidsagainstbullying.org
This interactive site has advice, games, contests, and kids' own stories about bullying.

Romain, Trevor. *Bullies Are a Pain in the Brain*. Minneapolis: Free Spirit Publications, 1997.
This illustrated book, also available on DVD, is a lighthearted look at bullying that offers sound, up-to-date advice.

Romain, Trevor. *Cliques, Phonies, and Other Baloney*. Minneapolis: Free Spirit Publications, 1998.
This book provides a humorous explanation of the difference between cliques and real friends. It's also available on DVD.

Simmons, Rachel. *Odd Girl Speaks Out.* San Diego: Harcourt, 2004.
This book is a collection of stories from girls about their personal experiences with bullies.

Index

Photo/Illustration Acknowledgments

The images in this book are used with the permission of: © Veer Haddon/Photonica/Getty Images, pp. 4, 48; © Henry King/Photonica/Getty Images, p. 6; © Maurice Ambler/Picture Post/Hulton Archive/Getty Images, p. 7; © Paul Morigi/WireImage/Getty Images, p. 10; AP Photo/Mark J. Terrill, p. 11; © Chris Clinton/Taxi/Getty Images, p. 12; AP Photo/Matt York, p. 13; © Baerbel Schmidt/Stone/Getty Images, pp. 14, 32; © age fotostock/SuperStock, pp. 15, 44, 54; © Julie Caruso, p. 17; © Ryan McVay/Taxi/Getty Images, pp. 18–19; © Nancy Honey/Photonica/Getty Images, p. 21; © David Madison/Riser/Getty Images, p. 22; © Dan Bigelow/The Image Bank/Getty Images, p. 23; © Mel Yates/Taxi/Getty Images, p. 24; © Sabine Duerichen/LOOK/Getty Images, p. 26; © Ray Pietro/Photonica/Getty Images, p. 28; AP Photo/Dan Steinberg, p. 29 (top); © Adrian Green/Stone/Getty Images, p. 29 (bottom); © Ableimages/Riser/Getty Images, pp. 31, 37; © Charlotte Nation/Stone/Getty Images, p. 34; © DCA Productions/Taxi/Getty Images, p. 36 (top); © Colin Gray/Photonica/Getty Images, p. 36 (bottom); © Roy Morsch/zefa/CORBIS, p. 39 (top); © Loungepark/The Image Bank/Getty Images, p. 39 (bottom); © CAP/Photonica/Getty Images, p. 41; © Michael Heinsen/Taxi/Getty Images, p. 42; © Charlotte Nation/Stone+/Getty Images, p. 47; © Rick Barrentine/CORBIS, p. 50; © Gideon Mendel/CORBIS, p. 53; © Kay Blaschke/Stock4B/Getty Images, p. 56; © Erin Patrice O'Brien/Taxi/Getty Images, p. 57.

Front cover: © Kwesi Hutchful/Hola Images/Getty Images.

About the Author

Carrie Golus has been a freelance writer since 1991. She has written hundreds of magazine and newspaper articles, as well as website content, brochures, video scripts, press releases, and the text for a museum exhibition. She holds a BA and a MA in English language and literature from the University of Chicago. Golus has self-published two comic books, both funded by grants. From 1998 to 2003, she and her husband, artist Patrick Welch, collaborated on the comic strip "Alternator," which ran in several alternative weekly newspapers. Her books include *Muhammad Ali* (Sports Heroes and Legends) and *Tupac Shakur* (Just the Facts). A native of Colorado, she lives in Chicago with her husband and twin boys.